American Life in the West

1800–1850

SADDLEBACK PUBLISHING

Saddleback's *Graphic American History*

ISBN-13: 978-1-59905-360-8
ISBN-10: 1-59905-360-8
eBook: 978-1-60291-688-3

Printed in Guangzhou, China
NOR/1012/CA21201344

16 15 14 13 12   5 6 7 8 9

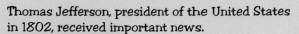

Thomas Jefferson, president of the United States in 1802, received important news.

There is no doubt about it, Mr. President. The rumor has been confirmed.

France has taken over New Orleans and the Louisiana Territory from Spain!

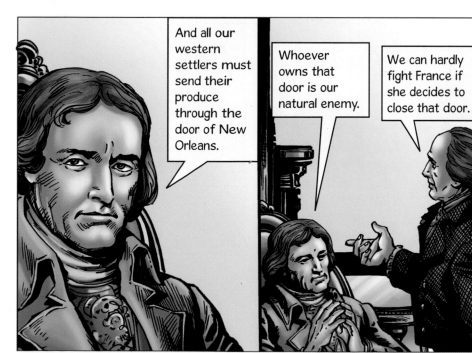

And all our western settlers must send their produce through the door of New Orleans.

Whoever owns that door is our natural enemy.

We can hardly fight France if she decides to close that door.

There might be another way! I will write to Robert Livingston. And I will send James Monroe to France to help Livingston.

In Paris a few weeks later Robert Livingston, minister to France, received a letter.

President Jefferson authorizes me to offer to buy New Orleans from the French! I must approach Talleyrand* very carefully.

A special messenger brought a unique commission to James Monroe.

This document makes me "Envoy Extraordinary and Minister Plenipoten-tiary" to both France and Spain.

What a grand title.

That is to flatter the French, and to impress them with my authority.

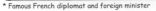

* Famous French diplomat and foreign minister

After long discussions with Jefferson and Madison, and hours of research, Monroe sailed for Paris.

Meanwhile Livingston, as instructed, opened negotiations with Talleyrand.

I am authorized to make an offer for the island of New Orleans.

Why not buy the whole of the Louisiana Territory?

Talleyrand usually spoke softly, and Livingston was a little deaf. Had he heard correctly?

I ... I beg your pardon sir. What did you say?

What will you give for the whole of Louisiana?

This was a tremendous development. Livingston pulled himself together. He must bargain!

Oh, no sir! I have no authority for that. And perhaps the United Stated is already too large.

We will talk again another day.

This was the amazing news that greeted Monroe when he arrived in Paris two days later.

Napoleon offers to sell us the whole of that great territory? And most of it still unexplored! Why would he do that?

He is on the edge of another war with England.

I see, I see! With the strong English navy between France and Louisiana, he stands to lose it any way.

So he might as well sell it and get something out of it! Exactly!

We are not authorized to buy so much—or to spend so much.

But to more than double our size—to remove all foreign interference from the Mississippi Valley—it is the opportunity of a lifetime!

Talks took place with Talleyrand. A price was agreed upon of $15 million—about four cents an acre. This was the biggest real estate deal in history!

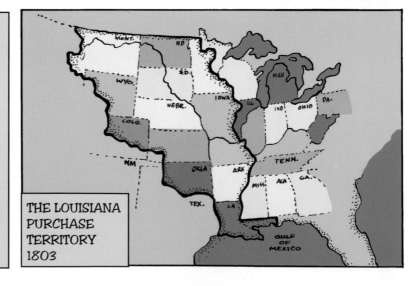

THE LOUISIANA PURCHASE TERRITORY 1803

In New Orleans on December 20, 1803, the French flag was lowered, the American flag was raised and the United States took possession of the Louisiana Territory!

Thomas Jefferson had great scientific curiosity. He had always wanted to know more about the western lands. Now they were part of the United States and still almost nothing was known about them.

Jefferson talked to young Meriwether Lewis, army captain.

We don't know about animal or plant life, geography, or the Indians. We don't even know the true boundaries!

I would like to send a small expedition to explore the territory.

I would like to accompany such an expedition, sir!

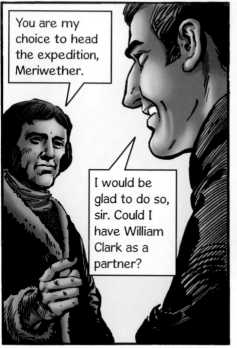

You are my choice to head the expedition, Meriwether.

I would be glad to do so, sir. Could I have William Clark as a partner?

He is a younger brother of George Rogers Clark and experienced in frontier life.

He sounds like a good choice. Pick your own men.

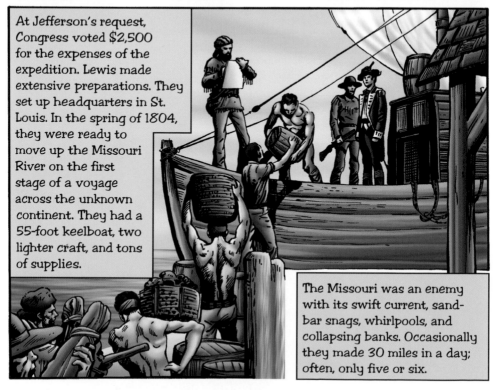

At Jefferson's request, Congress voted $2,500 for the expenses of the expedition. Lewis made extensive preparations. They set up headquarters in St. Louis. In the spring of 1804, they were ready to move up the Missouri River on the first stage of a voyage across the unknown continent. They had a 55-foot keelboat, two lighter craft, and tons of supplies.

The Missouri was an enemy with its swift current, sandbar snags, whirlpools, and collapsing banks. Occasionally they made 30 miles in a day; often, only five or six.

In addition to 28 soldiers and several boatmen, there were Clark's African-American servant, York, and Lewis's Newfoundland dog, Scammon.

The river provided all sorts of fish, including the biggest catfish they had ever seen.

We'll only report things as true that we've seen for ourselves.

One hundred twenty-six pounds! I've heard of 200 pounders.

They made notes of everything, this being one of the purposes of the trip.

There are hundreds of whooping cranes.

A cormorant!

The pelicans are comical!

Another important task was to observe the various kinds of Native Americans they met, and to make friends with them if possible—for these tribes were now inhabitants of the United States.

On May 22, they traded for fresh meat with a hunting party of friendly Kickapoos.

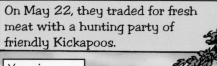

You give us four deer...

We give you two whiskeys!

Good! Good!

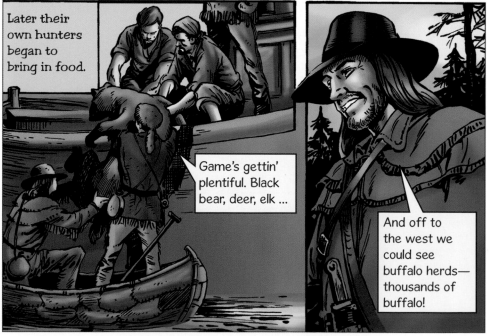

Later their own hunters began to bring in food.

Game's gettin' plentiful. Black bear, deer, elk ...

And off to the west we could see buffalo herds— thousands of buffalo!

On June 12 they met a raft headed south, loaded with furs and Frenchmen.

'Allo, Americaines! Bonjour monsieurs!

Greetings Frenchmen.

The two boats tied up for a visit. The captains wanted to learn everything possible about the trip ahead.

What about the Indians upriver?

High up you'll find the Mandans. They are good Indians. But before the Mandans you'll be in Sioux country!

And the Sioux?

The Sioux are sly, troublesome, and they'll demand gifts.

And there are thousands of them! You won't get through Sioux country without trouble.

As the Frenchmen had predicted, upriver the Sioux lined the river banks.

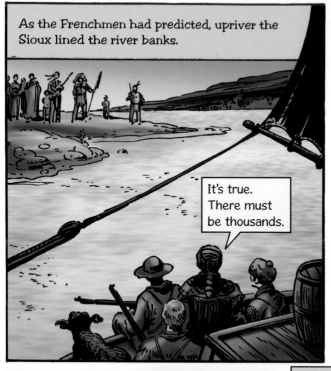

It's true. There must be thousands.

We must arrange a powwow* with them. That's part of our job.

Lewis and Clark went ashore with a small guard.

They were taken to the Sioux encampment, and Lewis made a speech.

We have come from the president in Washington. The French and Spanish have gone.

* A conference

We bring you American flags and medals. The president wants, his people to live in peace together...

They distributed gifts to the Sioux.

Then one of the chiefs stepped forward threateningly.

You insult us with cheap gifts! You must give much more. But no matter how much, you will not be allowed to go upriver.

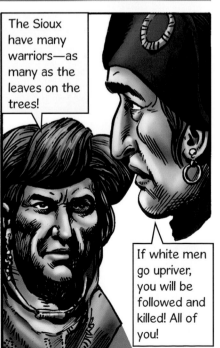

The Sioux have many warriors—as many as the leaves on the trees!

If white men go upriver, you will be followed and killed! All of you!

The moment was tense. Clark drew his sword, the guards raised their rifles.

We're Americans! This is our nation! We'll share it with you in peace and friendship, but if you try to bully us we'll wipe you off the earth!

Lewis and Clark withdrew safely to their boat. There they talked.

If we let them bully us, show any weakness, they'll attack.

And if they attack, we will be forced to defend ourselves and fight.

And though we could defend ourselves and withdraw safely, an attack means all-out war with the Sioux and the end of our mission!

First the Sioux chiefs threatened, then they begged. They came aboard, left again, tried to keep the boats from moving. The expedition was constantly on guard. When they moved upstream, the Indians followed along the banks for four days, but at last they disappeared.

They had been underway five months when they reached the Mandan villages.

It is mid-October. We have covered 1,600 miles!

Everyone tells us the Mandans are friendly.

We've had snow already, and ice along the riverbanks. We should make our winter encampment here.

They were welcomed by the Mandans. Cutting down cottonwood trees, they built their fort.

At times the temperature was 50 degrees below zero. When the weather permitted, they worked on dugout canoes.

On March 3 there was a welcome sight.

As the river narrows and becomes more shallow, we'll replace our big boats with these canoes.

Look! Ducks going north!

Spring is on its way.

Charbonneau, a French trapper, was in the Mandan village. He talked to Lewis.

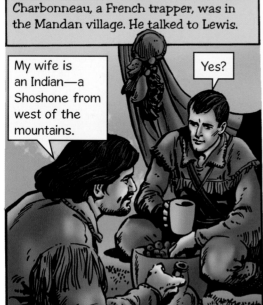

My wife is an Indian—a Shoshone from west of the mountains.

Yes?

Though captured as a child, she remembers the Shoshone language and some of the country. If we went with you, this might be helpful.

Indeed, yes! No one else knows Shoshone!

So it was that Sacagawea joined the expedition with her two-month-old baby.

I will be happy to travel back to the land of my father with you!

In April they started upriver again. Time after time they had to get out and push.

This is ice water!

The rocky bottom cuts my feet to pieces.

After months of difficult travel, they reached Montana and the Shoshone nation.

We must make them know we are friendly.

Where is Sacagawea?

Suddenly she rushed forward.

Do you not know me, my brother? I am your little sister, come home after all these winters!

I know you very well. Welcome home, little sister.

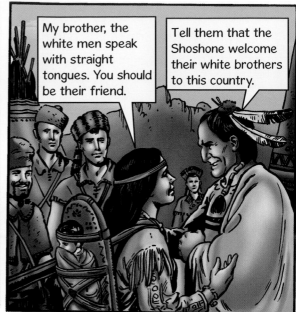

My brother, the white men speak with straight tongues. You should be their friend.

Tell them that the Shoshone welcome their white brothers to this country.

The expedition needed horses for crossing the Rocky Mountains. The Shoshones had horses, but only a few.

My brother, the white men must have horses.

We will let them have what they need.

Now came the most terrible time of all.

Don't ... know if I can make it!

You reckon it'll get much colder?

Hunger was what hurt the most. There was little game among the barren rocks.

You shoot anything?

Not enough to feed all our hungry people!

At last, on September 19, they staggered like scare-crows into a Nez Perce village.

Pray God they're friendly!

We can't look like much of a threat!

Tired, hungry, ill, they could not yet realize what they had accomplished. They had crossed the Rockies. They were near the headwaters of the Columbia River, on the last lap of their journey. The Nez Perce took them in, fed and cared for them.

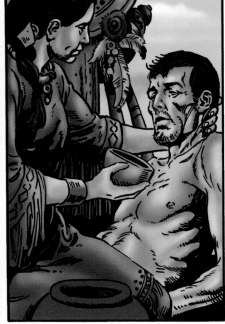

Soon they were strong enough to build new canoes, and to take to the swiftly flowing streams and rivers that would carry them, they hoped, to the Pacific Ocean.

Often they had to shoot rapids.

There were frequent detours around water too swift, or falls too high.

November 7 was a day of pouring rain and fog. Suddenly the fog rolled away.

Look! The Pacific Ocean!

We have reached the mouth of the Columbia and the western edge of the continent!

They built another fort and settled in. They named it Fort Clatsop for the nearby tribes.

If a ship arrives, at least some of us can return by sea.

The Indians have been asked to tell us if one anchors anywhere along this coast.

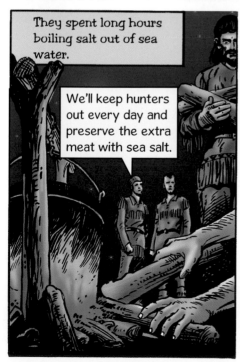

They spent long hours boiling salt out of sea water.

We'll keep hunters out every day and preserve the extra meat with sea salt.

The cold, rainy winter passed.

It is March again, but no ships!

I guess it's time to start back the way we came!

So they packed up and started back, up the swift rivers and over the mountains. Their experience helped them. They made a quicker and easier trip. At last they reached the Missouri again and the Mandan village, where they parted from Charbonneau, Sacagawea, and the baby Baptiste, now old enough to do a baby war dance.

We can never thank you enough, Sacagawea, for your help.

When the little dancing boy is old enough, bring him to St. Louis and we will send him to school!

On September 23, 1806, they paddled into the town of St. Louis at the mouth of the Missouri.

Thomas Jefferson and the country would say much more about it.

It is over! Eight thousands miles, and we are back.

It was a good trip.

It was wonderful, a miracle! You proved the size of the territory, the wealth of it, the variety! A man could study your journey for a lifetime!

Any by descending the Columbia River to the sea, you've given us our strongest claim on Oregon!

In 1808, by request, Albert Gallatin made a report to Congress.

I recommend that the national government build a series of roads and canals connecting the East and the West.

Congress took action.

I propose the appropriation of enough money to construct a national road from Cumberland, Maryland, to St. Louis, Missouri.

The bill was passed and came to President Jefferson.

Will you sign it or veto it?

Is it constitutional for the government to do such construction work? I doubt it.

But think what such a road would mean to the settlement of the West. I'll sign it.

Construction began using a new process invented by a John McAdam.

It's called a macadamized* road. The more traffic, the better it gets!

The National or Cumberland Road, today U. S. 40, was a success, Carrying traffic at the rate of 10 miles an hour, an amazing improvement over any other road we had, it greatly increased the flow of western traffic.

This used to be a quiet country road.

Seems as if everybody in the world's moving west.

* A road with a multilayered surface of crushed stone.

On August 9, 1807, people along the Hudson River in New York State watched a great event.

When'll it get here, Dad?

Maybe never, Son! Some call it Fulton's Folly.

Explain it again. I can't get it in my head how it works.

Why, there's a boat with a steam engine on it—and the engine turns a paddle wheel—and that makes the boat move.

Look! Something's coming!

Yippee! Look at it go!

Wonderful! No sails, no oars. It's a new age beginning!

Robert Fulton's *Clermont,* averaging five miles an hour, went upstream from New York to Albany in 32 hours.

DeWitt Clinton, governor of New York, was quick to see the possibilities.

These steamboats will revolutionize river travel!

Yes?

They can carry goods up and down the Ohio and the Mississippi, between Lake Erie and New Orleans—and between the port of New York and Albany.

With a waterway across the state connecting us with the West, New York could become the greatest port in the country!

In 1817, New York authorized the building of a canal 363 miles long. Not everyone favored it.

What're they building?

That's Clinton's ditch. Fool idea! Supposed to connect up the Hudson River with Lake Erie.

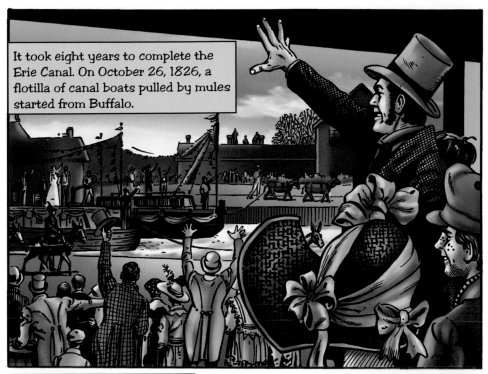

It took eight years to complete the Erie Canal. On October 26, 1826, a flotilla of canal boats pulled by mules started from Buffalo.

In every village the mules were startled by cheering crowds.

Hurrah! Three cheers for the Erie Canal! Hurrah for Clinton's ditch.

The lead boat carried two kegs of water from Lake Erie to New York. Clinton poured the lake water into the sea as cannons fired a salute.

The canal was a great success. At once freight rates dropped from $100 a ton to $8. It made New York a great city and carried thousands of passengers west.

The first railroad in the United States was a little horsedrawn line, opened in Quincy, Massachusetts, in 1826.

They've found horses can haul a much heavier load on rails than on a road.

That's progress!

Then someone figured out how to put a steam engine in a locomotive.

There's no doubt of it—railroads are the transportation of the future!

Sort of an "iron horse"?

In 1828, the Baltimore and Ohio Railroad Company started building tracks. It was slow work.

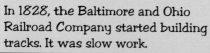

In 1830, the Baltimore and Ohio put its first small locomotive into service. It was called Tom Thumb.

How long has this been going on?

Two years, and they built only 14 miles of track.

By 1850 there would be 9,000 miles of track connecting the major cities of the East and carrying goods and people between the East and the West.

St. Louis, on the frontier, was the gateway to the West. Lewis and Clack started and ended their trip there. In 1819, William Ashley, lieutenant governor of Missouri, went into a St. Louis newspaper office.

I want to advertise for men, energetic young men, to ascend the Missouri River.

Yes sir, General Ashley!

You starting a new venture?

Just planning to do a little business in furs.

The venture would become the Ashley Rocky Mountain Fur Company. And among the men Ashley interviewed were names that would change the future of the West. One of them was Jim Beckwourth.

You're a good shot and fair blacksmith, but you've never done trapping before?

That's right, General.

ASHLEY ROCKY MOUNTAIN FUR COMPANY

It's tough work. It can be dangerous and you'll be snowbound all winter in the wilderness!

I'd like to try it.

Jed Smith, Jim Bridger, Bill Sublette, Tom Fitzpatrick—these were the other men who would try it, some with companies, some as loners. In their love of wilderness and their search for valuable furs, they would explore the West to the Pacific, find the passes through the mountains, and open the way for the settlers who would follow. They were the Mountain Men.

They rode across the Kansas plains, crossed the mouth of the Platte River, and turned north along the Missouri River.

By mid-September they reached their first destination, the Pawnee Camp at Ottumwa.

It's a busy place!

They're getting ready for the buffalo surround.

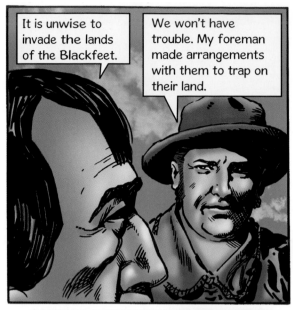

It is unwise to invade the lands of the Blackfeet.

We won't have trouble. My foreman made arrangements with them to trap on their land.

We can spare no braves until after the run! But wait and join us in the hunt. Then we can offer you *pemmican** as a gift for the tools you have brought us.

It's been a long time since I've seen one. Tom? Jim?

It's all right with me.

I've never seen one.

The men can use a rest after the trek from St. Louis. Two Axe, we accept your invitation.

Good! Our scouts say the herd will be on the Oahe Plains shortly.

* A concentrated food of pounded and dried meat mixed with melted fat.

In the morning, Jim Beckwourth watched the final preparations.

They ride the workhorses to keep their ponies fresh for the charge.

The dogs will pull the empty travoises* to the hunt. Then the workhorses will pull the loaded travoises back to the village afterwards.

Come. We will watch the surround from ridge.

Like an army, the caravan of mounted braves, yelping dogs, and supporting women moved across the grassy plains.

* For carrying loads

For two hours the crowd moved north. Then in the distance two scouts appeared.

The herd lies two leagues north on the Oahe Plains. A large one!

We can drive them between the ridges.

Is there danger of driving then over the cliffs?

No, we will kill all we need before the herd reaches the cliffs.

Take your braves and circle the herd from the ridges.

Bands of hunters, now on their fastest ponies, moved quietly toward the nearby ridges.

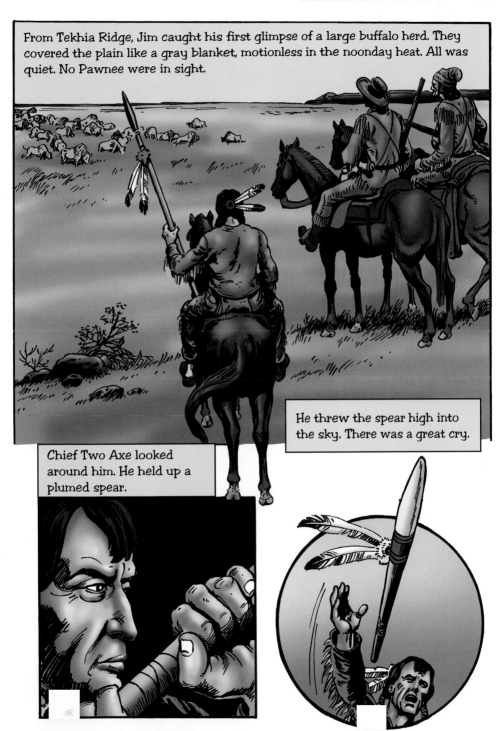

From Tekhia Ridge, Jim caught his first glimpse of a large buffalo herd. They covered the plain like a gray blanket, motionless in the noonday heat. All was quiet. No Pawnee were in sight.

He threw the spear high into the sky. There was a great cry.

Chief Two Axe looked around him. He held up a plumed spear.

Even before the spear curved downward, the ridges exploded with life. Indian braves rode toward the buffalo from three sides with screeching cries and galloping hoofbeats. The buffalo bolted. The stampede was on!

Holding his spear with one hand, his pony's mane with the other, each brave crisscrossed into the mass of buffalo.

Singling out one animal, each hunter skillfully drove his spear into the vital neck area.

Now the women will load the meat and take it to the drying scaffolds.

You see how they hang it up there?

They'll keep the fires going all night, smoking and drying the meat.

Guests and workers alike feasted on buffalo.

Best meat I ever tasted.

Nothing like fresh buffalo meat.

The next morning the women pounded the dried meat into powder, mixed it with spices and berries, coated it with melted buffalo fat, and packed it into buffalo-skin cases.

So that's pemmican! How does it taste?

Next winter, when game's scarce, you'll think it tastes fine.

Next day the party left the Indian village.

Goodbye Two Axe. See you next spring.

Good hunting.

At Fort Clark, Ashley divided the party into six groups, each with a different territory.

All right men, we'll meet back here on April 1. Good luck!

Jim went with Ashley, Fitzpatrick, Lajeunesse, and a Pawnee guide. They rode into the eastern Rockies.

How far have we come?

Maybe 300 miles.

Suddenly from behind there was a commotion.

She slipped! That's our food!

Quickly the mule was swept away.

All our food was on that mule!

We're at least a week from Fort Clark.

We can't make it without food. We must hunt.

They camped that night without food. In the morning, snow was in the air.

All right, men let's go.

To find game, you must go beyond the forest.

The Indian stays here to guard the animals. The rest of us will go off in four directions.

If you kill anything, fire two shots. We'll come back here, and if it's something big, we'll all go to carry it in.

Jim started in the directions Ashley told him.

He walked for hours, stopping only to cut blazes.

He felt a tremor. He put his ear to the ground.

Antelope! I'm sure of it.

Pushing forword warily, he came out onto high grassland.

They're so fast! Could I possibly get two?

He took out two bullets. He fired, reloaded, fired again.

I did it!

Night came and passed. At camp the other men worried.

I hope Jim's not lost or too weak from hunger to get back here!

We'd better look for him. He doesn't know this country.

Weak from cold and hunger, the men followed Jim's trail. Finally they smelled smoke.

Jim! Why didn't you come back? We were worried.

No use making two trips. I knew you'd find me!

And it'll take all of us to carry back the meat! Now come and eat!

Enough meat for two weeks! We're saved!

Well supplied with meat, Lajeunesse was able to make the trip back to Fort Clark for supplies while the others went on to the winter camp.

Good winter camp here!

We'll get our cabin built and our traps out.

Despite snow and cold, the winter passed quickly. Every day there were chores.

The traps had to be set and the catch removed.

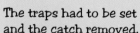

The trapped beavers were skinned and the skins dressed.

A roaring fire kept the cabin warm.

On April 1, they were back at Fort Clark to meet the other mountain men.

Good work, men! This is the best season ever!

Yep! Each year we go further into the mountains 'n' trap more furs. Wonder if we're ruining ourselves!

We find the way—and behind us come the settlers with their wagons and plows. Someday us and the wilderness is gonna be pushed into the Pacific Ocean!

Nonsense, man! Nobody's gonna get wagons and women over the Rockies!

But Tom Fitzpatrick himself, a few years later, led the first women and the first wagon over the Rockies into Oregon through the South Pass discovered by other Ashley men.

In Rushville, New York, in December 1835, the church service was ready to begin. Suddenly three strangers entered.

Why, its Dr. Marcus Whitman back from the West!

The one engaged to Narcissa Prentiss?

Not only were Marcus and Narcissa deeply in love, but they shared the same ambition.

They were married and on March 3, 1836, they left homes and families to begin the long trip to Oregon.

It is true! The Indians beyond the Rockies are calling for the gospel. The church will send us together to teach them.

We will do God's work together!

God keep you till we meet again.

Goodbye! Goodbye!

They went by steamboat to Cincinnati, to St. Louis, and to Liberty, Missouri, the end of the line. With them went two Native American boys and two other missionaries, Eliza and Henry Spalding.

The company boat will pick us up here and take us on to Council Bluffs where we'll meet the caravan.

After ten days wait, they heard the company steamer on the river.

Stop! Wait!

Sorry—no room for more passengers.

There was only one thing to do. Whitman bought riding horses, a wagon for luggage, and they took off across the prairie.

There were dangerous rivers to ford.

Don't worry Marcus—we'll make it!

After days of hard riding, the greenhorns met the first challenge and overtook the fur caravan. Its leader was Tom Fitzpatrick.

You've given us the honor, ma'am, of being the first brigade ever to take a white woman over the mountains.

Through the heat and dust, the caravan followed the river Platte.

They say the Platte is a thousand miles long and six inches deep.

On the treeless plain, Narcissa and Eliza learned to make fires of buffalo chips.*

Fresh buffalo meat every day, what a luxury!

I fear it does not agree with me.

After two months, they were riding through South Pass, gateway to Oregon. Just beyond was the fur trapper's rendezvous.

What is a rendezvous, Tom?

Why ma'am, it's where the trappers get together to enjoy themselves after a hard winter.

They'll sell their furs ... eat and drink and play cards ... some of them'll spend in a few days all the money they've worked all winter to make!

More important to the Whitmans, the rendezvous was the end of the trail for the fur caravan.

I've met two English fur traders from the Hudson Bay Company. Perhaps they'll let us go on to Oregon with them.

* dried buffalo manure

The Englishmen McLeod and Mackay discussed the matter.

We don't want American trappers in Oregon—or American settlers!

But missionaries to the Indians are a different matter. Why not give them our help?

McLeod did not know that he was taking a big step toward losing Oregon for his country.

They set out with the English party. Six weeks travel over the roughest part of the trail lay ahead.

They call these the Blue Mountains.

They're very beautiful and very steep!

The last part of the journey was down the Columbia River.

What a thrilling ride.

At Fort Vancouver, they were greeted by the British agent, Dr. McLoughlin.

Why are all the flags flying? Is it a holiday?

Ah, Madame, we are honoring the first white women ever to descend the Columbia!

The Whitmans started a mission among the Cayuse Indians at a spot near Walla Walla, Washington, called Waiilatpu.

I will soon build furniture and add more rooms.

Our parents must have made a similar start in Western New York.

The Sunday services the Whitmans held were well attended by the Cayuse.

The children came daily to Narcissa's school classes.

Indian sign here. English word here!

RIVERS
BIRDS
BUFFALO
MOON

Whitman delighted in the rich soil.

I am going to plant wheat and corn. I'll build a grist mill.

I'd like to see this land filled with neat farms and happy families—American families.

The Whitmans and others sent word back East of the wonders of Oregon. In September 1842, a band of settlers just over the mountains arrived.

Welcome to Waiilatpu!

Am I pleased, white folks and houses! We had to leave the wagons at Snake Fort, but 112 of us made it with horses and pack mules!

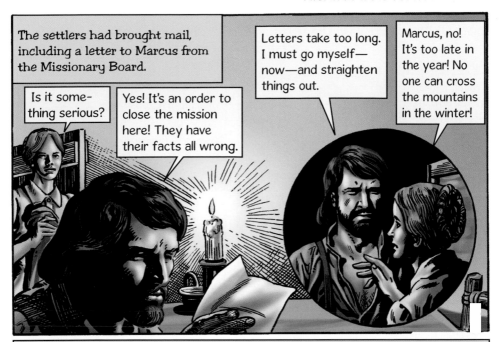

The settlers had brought mail, including a letter to Marcus from the Missionary Board.

Is it something serious?

Yes! It's an order to close the mission here! They have their facts all wrong.

Letters take too long. I must go myself—now—and straighten things out.

Marcus, no! It's too late in the year! No one can cross the mountains in the winter!

But Marcus was determined. He would save the mission—and he would do more! He would go to Washington, see the president, convince the politicians that this was the time to claim Oregon for the United States!

He found a man who would go with him. They set off on October 3, 1842.

Goodbye. God bless you and keep you.

Alone in her rooms, she read the Bible and thought.

It will be at least a year before I know whether he made it through the mountains or died. It is right that he should go!

HOLY Bible

In May 1848, a great wagon train gathered at Independence, Missouri, ready to roll West: two thousand animals, a thousand people, a hundred wagons. They kept turning to one man for advice, Marcus Whitman.

Travel, travel, travel, nothing else will take you to the end of your journey! Nothing is good that causes a moment's delay!

When there were rivers to ford, he rode across first, finding a firm bottom.

They passed the great prairie landmarks.

SCOTT'S BLUFF

CHIMNEY ROCKS

INDEPENDENCE ROCK

At Fort Hall in September, they were told by the British commander to leave their wagons there.

It's impossible to take wagons through! You'll be lucky to make it with horses without starving to death!

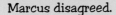

Marcus disagreed.

Stick to your wagons and oxen. You'll need them for farming. If we pull together, we can haul the wagons through in spite of high water!

Take the wagons! On to Oregon! Oregon for the Americans!

The Snake was the worst river yet, swift, wide, and deep. They chained the wagons together.

Now all together.

Men went ahead to make the mountain trails passable.

If there was no other way, they lifted the wagons over.

But they made it. A thousand settlers and a hundred wagons had come over the Oregon Trail safely. Many more would follow.

In the spring of 1846, the emigrants who came over the Rockies brought disturbing news.

God's angels watched over you and brought you home!

The treaty of joint occupation is ended! Britain and the United States won't share the territory together any longer.

But which will Oregon be—British or American?

Don't know. It wasn't settled when we left. There could be war!

In the Columbia River at Oregon City, two war ships waited: the British *Modeste* and the American *Shark*.

In the late winter of 1847, a ship arrived from Hawaii carrying Honolulu newspapers.

Any news?

News ... *news?*

A treaty was signed with England last June. Right up to Puget Sound all land south of the 49th parallel is American!

In Oregon City, the people went wild with excitement. The American flag was raised. Cannons fired from the *Shark.*